CARE FOR THE
NEURODIVERGENT
SOUL
Companion Workbook

A Guide for The Soulful, Sensitive, and Brilliantly Wired

DIANNE A. ALLEN, MA

VISIONS APPLIED

For permission requests, write to the publisher at:
Visions Applied, LLC
www.visionsapplied.com
www.msdianneallen.com

ISBN: 978-1-968943-01-1

Library of Congress Control Number: 2025921300

Cover design by Nic Albright

Interior design by Clark Kenyon
Printed in the United States of America

First Edition

Neurodivergent—Mental health. 2. Giftedness—Self-care. 3. Emotional well-being. I. Title.

Dedication

To Cole and Jud Cummings, gifted and talented brothers who exemplify courage. When it comes to perseverance and diligence in working on themselves, they are following in their parents' footsteps and embracing their neurodivergence in beautiful and powerful ways. Cole and Jud, you inspire me and much of the focus for this project. Your lights shine so beautifully, and I am honored to know you. With deep love and respect.

Contents

Introduction - A Note from Me to You

Greetings,

I'm so glad you're here.

To the adventurer in you who is the outlier. You are on a treasure hunt. Each false belief or idea that you release and rectify brings you more peace and satisfaction in life. More importantly, self-compassion and care for your neurodivergent soul becomes the very treasure you are yearning to experience.

If you're holding this workbook, I already know something about you, you are someone who is ready to care for yourself in a deeper, more intentional way. You are honoring who you've always been as you care for you.

This companion workbook was born out of love, love for your neurodivergent soul, love for your messy, beautiful process of healing and transformation. Herein lies a roadmap toward your freedom from what holds you back while you also are creating the deeply connected life you deserve.

I created this as a space where you can land softly, speak honestly, and build a life that feels like it truly fits. You have likely spent too long trying to squeeze yourself into spaces or systems that were never designed with you in mind. That stops here.

This is your space to explore and to remember who you truly are. Remember, you are not too much. You are not broken. You are wired for something powerful and inspiring.

Everything in this workbook is an invitation for you to expand into more and more of your authentic self. Go at your pace. Skip around. Come back when you feel the calling to revisit aspects. No wrong way to work with this workbook and you cannot mess this up! You are not late either!

As you move through these pages, know that I'm walking with you. Every word is infused with deep care, respect, intention, and hard-won truth. This is the work I've done and continue to do because I know the freedom you can experience is very real.

You deserve support that *gets* you and I get you. You deserve care that actually nourishes you. You deserve to live without apology, without burnout, and without constantly wondering if you're doing life "right." You're already doing the most important thing: showing up for yourself.

As you transform old limiting beliefs and actions into higher, aligned beliefs, words and actions, everyone benefits, most importantly you! Let's keep going.

With deep love and unwavering belief in you,

Dianne

How to Use This Workbook

This is your space, your soft landing, your brave container, your mirror, and your map. This workbook is here to help you explore, express, and care for your neurodivergent soul, not to fix you, not to change who you are, but to help you come home to yourself. Here's how to make the most of this companion workbook:

1. Start with the Book
Begin by reading *Care for the Neurodivergent Soul*. Let the words sink in. Let your nervous system guide you. Take your time to reflect when you wish.

2. Reflect in Your Own Way
Starting in Part 4 of this workbook, each chapter pairs with a chapter from *Care for the Neurodivergent Soul*. You'll find reflection questions, journaling prompts, sensory cues, and exercises designed to meet you where you are. Write, draw, doodle, voice-note, collage, whatever helps your thoughts take shape.

3. Create a Space that Feels Safe
Find or create a sensory-friendly environment to do this work. Think soft lighting, soothing textures, a favorite drink, or a stim object. The space you choose should make you feel held, not judged. You will find more ideas and suggestions in the personal journal section near the back of the book.

4. Honor Your Unique and Personal Rhythm
There are no deadlines, no grades, no right or wrong answers. Go at your pace. Skip around. Come back later. Your timing is sacred.

5. Be Honest, Be Gentle
Let this be a place where you can speak your truth in a raw, tender, joyful, messy or even logical manner. Meet your inner world with compassion and love rather than comparison and judgment.

6. Revisit and Repeat
You'll grow through cycles. What resonates today may evolve tomorrow. Use this workbook again and again. Let it change with you.

This is a soul conversation.

Let it hold you. Let it challenge you. Let it reflect the beauty of your wiring.

You're brilliant. You are different by design.
I believe in you.

Foreword

Care for the Neurodivergent Soul Companion Workbook is a beacon of empowerment for neurodivergent individuals, offering you a much-needed space to embrace and celebrate your unique gifts without apology. What makes this workbook truly special is its ability to guide you through the complexities of overcoming the pressures often placed on those of us with special abilities. The pressures of daily life that often demand conformity, self-doubt, and the suppression of your inherent strengths can take a toll on your peace, happiness, and joy. Dianne encourages you to step into your power with unapologetic confidence, leaving hesitation and self-doubt behind.

The workbook provides you with practical, heartfelt exercises designed to help you recognize and fully access your innate gifts. You may have been overlooking or invalidating these gifts in similar ways to the world which often overlooks or misunderstands you and your neurodiversity. Dianne doesn't just encourage self-acceptance; she pushes you to own who you are, to stop shrinking for the comfort of others, and to unapologetically embrace your unique way of being. She shares a powerful message that resonates deeply with anyone who has ever felt pressured to fit into a box that was not made for them.

From thoughtful reflections to actionable steps, this workbook gently, yet firmly, guides you on a journey of self-discovery and empowerment. It reminds you that being neurodivergent is something beautiful and powerful to be celebrated. For anyone looking to break free from the constraints of society's expectations and stand tall in their brilliance, *Care for the Neurodivergent Soul Companion Workbook* is a must-have. It is a declaration of unapologetic confidence inviting you to live powerfully in your own skin.

Anna Lohr, BSW

Preface

You are brilliantly wired.
You are deeply aware.
You are worthy of care that honors your design.
This workbook exists to support your journey home to yourself.

Care for the Neurodivergent Soul was written to speak directly to the soulful, sensitive, and visionary part of you, the part that feels everything deeply and sees more than most. This companion workbook is where that part gets to breathe, explore, and shine.

Inside these pages, you'll find space to reflect, to create, and to connect with your own wisdom. Each prompt, exercise, and practice is here to help you recognize your rhythm, align with your values, and expand your sense of possibility.

You may discover new insights. You may uncover patterns that are ready to shift. You may feel more seen, more grounded, and more yourself with each page. That's the power of intentional reflection and soulful care.

Your mind, body, and spirit already carry the answers. This workbook simply helps you tune in and listen more closely.

Move at your own pace. Choose your own way. Use the tools that speak to you and let the rest wait. This is your space. This is your time.

Thank you for bringing your energy, your truth, and your commitment to this work. I'm honored to walk alongside you.

With deep respect,

Dianne A. Allen, MA

GETTING STARTED

Basic Beliefs

Everyone has a set of operating beliefs, both conscious and unconscious. These beliefs instruct how we think, feel, see and act in the world. Caring for your neurodivergent soul includes taking the time to focus within and beginning to uncover the hidden obstacles.

Think of your care as an unfolding beautiful experience where there is always something new and exciting to discover. There is no finish line when it comes to caring for our inner world. We are always evolving and tending to our personal needs.

Taking steps in manageable ways and making a commitment to yourself to continue your learning and growth, you embark on this project. Here are the 11 steps that will help guide you as you continue in this workbook and elsewhere in your life.

Awareness

I believe that becoming aware is the initial step in making any change or transition. Sometimes the awareness is merely a discontent or a sense that "something isn't right or that there must be more." Maybe your awareness is that your particular neurodivergence is causing challenges in your life and you are ready to find a new way to approach your life that will yield powerful results and more satisfaction. Simply having awareness that there is an issue of some type is a vital first step.

Honesty

Telling yourself the truth about the actual state of affairs within is crucial to your transformation and care of your soul. This requires looking beneath the mask or façade and being willing to tell the truth. This can be challenging and is often why having trusted others is important. I find that often having a trusted other who is not related to you is vital. Sometimes the love for you may color the response you receive from a loved one. The love actually can skew things. As you become more aware, keep telling the truth. As things are uncovered or revealed, being honest must come next.

Open mindedness

Being open minded and open hearted are essential elements for your care and transformation. As Einstein said: "You can't solve a problem with the same thinking that created it." Though your life is not a problem to be fixed, the idea that our old ways of thinking do not bring in the new ways of thinking, speaking and acting is a valid one.

Willingness to Change

You must be willing to let go of the parts of you that are no longer serving. . The principle here is to release the old and then trust in the arrival of the new. Too many people try to hold onto the old while gathering the new, and they leave no room for their growth, so they end up stuck. Your willingness must include releasing the old so you can receive the new. This includes beliefs, thoughts, words, actions, people, and opportunities.

Taking Stock

As you move through your life, it is important to stop and take stock of the state of affairs. How are you feeling? What is important to you currently? It is a good idea to journal your progress and awareness to be able to track your progress and identify obstacles.

Telling Your Truth

Having trusted others is vital. We are often taught to or believe that we must do everything alone. I have heard thousands of times "You're smart, you know what to do. Figure it out." Well, what if the answers we seek are on our soul level and not simply mental exercises? It is mandatory to have someone with whom you can share your thoughts and ideas while practicing new behaviors and boundaries. Preferably the trusted others have awareness and understanding. It is vital that you speak your innermost truth as you trust more and more so that you gain perspective as you move along. This can be very hard and feels vulnerable, and it is. Yet, these connections and risks are what make your neurodivergent life satisfying and fulfilling.

Shining the light on the obstacles

Only light can expel the darkness. When you enter a dark room and turn on the light, the darkness leaves. By definition, the lower beliefs that need to be expelled are lower vibrations and they ought to be replaced. Lower beliefs are the beliefs that you are operating with that are outdated and therefore holding you back. By replacing outdated (lower) beliefs with more desirable and effective ones, you can transcend many obstacles that once seemed insurmountable.

Creating a plan to navigate and rectify them

As a neurodivergent person you may resist plans or the making plans. I understand. I do sometimes as well, yet making some sort of plan for your freedom and care is vital. Always reserve the right to change your mind and alter the plan. Still, have a plan for your self-care that includes all major life areas.

Taking Focused Action

Focused action yields powerful results. You may have trouble with delayed gratification. You may want to feel the incredible results of caring for your neurodivergent soul. As you become more empowered and confident, your focused action affords you the results you are seeking and more. This or something better.

Being Open to Feedback

Feedback loops are essential for your happiness and reaching your goals of any kind. The more frequently you seek feedback the more positive results you attain. Being open to feedback from trusted others and from your own life's results can help you change your course if you need to quickly and with calm assurance.

Offering Support and Wisdom to Others

As you become proficient in caring for your neurodivergent soul, you will feel the inner compelling to share your experience with others who are seeking. As you are open minded and willing, others will want to learn from you. Here is where we remember that serving others also serves you.

The circle continues with more awareness and so on, ad infinitum. You will find yourself walking these steps at a varied pace in different times of your life. The key here, I believe, is paying attention and being honest with yourself, really. From this place of inner honesty, you are invited to surround yourself with trusted others to listen, love and guide you. Remember, you are living your life and therefore cannot be fully objective. Having someone who can see what you cannot see is a vital part of your success. Sometimes, when a blind spot is revealed, it stings like ripping off a band-aid. It is in the uncovering of the wound that allows the healing to take place. The sting eventually leaves, and you are left with more freedom and happiness that you can now share with others.

The Benefits

You have most likely been reading and learning about neurodivergence. You are a living example of the nuance and complexity that lies within you. These variances show up in the world and being different by design affords you the opportunity to embrace the beauty and power of your neurodivergence in your life. Let's look at some of the benefits in doing the work in this workbook and beyond.

Healing Past Pains

Imagine having a dull, constant ache that you can handle but which never fully leaves you alone. Even when you are not paying attention to this ache, it continues to steal vital resources because your mind, body and emotions are having to moderate the ache even when you are not paying direct attention to the ache. Taking the time and investing your energy in clearing old pains is relieving these old aches and pains that have been around for much too long. For many of you, the conspicuous absence of the nagging pain will be noticeable. You don't know how bad your pain level was until there is relief. Carrying around old pain and grief is tiresome and takes much more energy than you may realize. This workbook will offer you avenues to explore for your [personal relief.

Living Your Purpose on Purpose

You will be able to be you in all your glory, messiness, and quirkiness. Your purpose and inner heart's desire is meant for you to live with authenticity. As you embrace your genuine self and you allow your innermost vision to begin to show up, your clarity, conviction, and focus will help lead the way for a fulfilling and satisfying life. Your vision and purpose did not come through like a conference call. Your purpose and vision is unique to you and you alone. You are here to live your unique purpose on purpose. You are not meant to do it alone.

Self-Understanding

One of your desires, most likely, is to learn more and more about your inner workings and how you can become increasingly aware on many levels. By taking a deep dive into your neurodivergent soul and taking exquisite care of you, your inherent power emerges in meaningful ways. I bet in ways you never thought possible.

Experiencing Your Wholeness

You may have heard me say before that "You are Perfect, Whole, and Complete." I believe that you live with your inner light dimmed to some extent, that you experience an form of existential grief. You inherently know that there is something missing in your life. The more you care for your neurodivergent soul, the brighter your light can emerge in healthy and empowering ways.

Improved Authentic Relationships

I am talking about all relationships. Your relationship with yourself, others around you, the environment, and the world at large. The more you peel away the parts that do not serve your highest good, the more authentically you can engage with your world from the inside out. You are freer in your engagements. Projecting your pain and old grievances onto others disappears, and you begin to trust yourself even more day to day.

Enhanced Innovation and Creativity

Your visionary self gets to come out and play. Your inner clarity becomes obvious and the fog lifts. Staying stuck because it is comfortable and you know the rules become old news and your natural curiosity takes center stage. Your channels are clear and your discernment keen.

Improved Emotional Resilience

As you explore, identify, and integrate your many aspects of self, you develop improved resilience. Life will continue to happen, and many things are out of your control. Your nervous system is designed for heightened awareness so integrating new information, beliefs, and patterns that serve you and your health are vital. The more you care for your soul, the more emotional resilience you develop. You are able to rebound after challenges more effectively.

Deeper Spiritual Connection

Your spiritual connection is about setting yourself free of old bondage that comes through in beliefs, attitudes, and behaviors. Many of these old bindings were not created by you and may not serve you today. You are the one who gets to decide what works best for you. You get to decide how to live your deeper calling in concert with others. Your connection and your ability to feel and experience your connection with the grater Universe is essential when caring for your neurodivergent soul. The more depth you nurture, the more authentic soul power and presence you emanate. This changes your inner life and circumstances because you are more deeply connected to life herself.

A Sense of Inner Competence

The more you trust in your process and remember that your life is precious, the more you are free to create the life you have imagined and more. It all starts with being willing to tell the truth and then being willing to trust. Trust means to have "consistency over time." The more you care for your neurodivergent soul, the more competence you experience and more your trust and so on. When you are standing in your sovereignty, you will know that the work has been well worth the dark nights and the triumphs.

My Letter of Commitment

Take some time and read the following letter of commitment and add your personal touch or write your own letter. It is important to have your commitment in writing so you can reflect on your intention. Below is an example of a letter you may use or use the next page to write your own. Be sure to sign and date the letter.

Dear _____ **Date:** _____

This is my promise to you, from you.

Starting today, I commit to honoring the way my mind works, not as something to fix, hide, or overcome, but as something to understand, protect, and celebrate.

I will stop measuring myself against standards that were never built with me in mind. I will stop treating my needs as inconveniences. I will stop apologizing for being wired differently. My brain is not broken. My pace, my patterns, my sensitivities, my intensity are not flaws. They are facts. They are me.

I will learn what supports me and give myself those things without guilt. Rest, quiet, stimulation, structure, freedom, whatever I need, I will listen and respond with care, not criticism.

I will no longer shove myself into boxes just to make others comfortable. I am not here to perform normally. I am here to live fully. Authentically. Sustainably.

This is not a short-term effort. This is not a phase. This is a lifelong relationship with myself, and with the truth of who I am.

While this journey may be messy and nonlinear, I'm not walking away from myself ever again. I will show up for me. I will choose compassion over shame. I will choose understanding over judgment. I choose to believe that I am worthy of care right here and now.

This is my commitment. I've got me.

With Deep Love and Respect,

_____   _____

[Your Name]   Date

I am a wild current, a quiet storm with a different kind of shine.
From this moment on, I will shine, shine, shine.

WHO ARE YOU AND WHAT DO YOU BELIEVE?

In this part, I invite you to take a look at yourself and your beliefs about the world and how it all works. You want to begin to discern what you believe is working so those beliefs can be retained and reinforced. The beliefs that are not currently working for you can then be replaced with new beliefs that work more effectively for your life and happiness.

As a neurodivergent soul, the world can be tricky, confusing and at times painful or scary. The goal in this part is to go a bit deeper into how your beliefs are shaping your self-talk, words, and actions. Those beliefs that are currently limiting you can be replaced with ones that are more suitable for your unique, expansive nature.

Start by writing down a list of your beliefs regarding topics such as the ones below and add others as well. Be sure to have at least 3 things listed for each word. Explore your innermost beliefs and be honest with yourself as this is for your welfare and satisfaction. There are no wrong answers.

Women:

Men:

Non-Binary:

Neurodivergent:

Neurotypical:

Love:

Fear:

Success:

Failure:

Satisfaction:

Emotions/Feelings:

Self-care:

_____

_____

_____

You may have already noticed some beliefs that do not seem to suit you anymore. This is great news. This is where you can start to lovingly release what is no longer serving to create space for what will serve you much better.

Do you notice any belief conflicts that are operating within you that you did not notice before? We will move forward to releasing the old and reinforce what serves you while creating new, more contemporary beliefs for your current and future success and happiness.

Let's start with your unique story. Your story is valuable and meaningful. All the ups and downs, people, places, and experiences all create the unique fabric of your life. The rich, vibrant colors and textures intermingled with the dark or other contrasting experiences are yielding you beautiful tapestry. Every experience and decision and action has led you to this time; reading this book and making decisions to benefit your future self. Congratulations on creating the time and space to honor your unique life.

Exercise: Honoring your story

The good, the bad, the ugly and the magnificent

Take the time to write a thoughtful story of your life. The idea here is to recollect experiences and memories for more understanding of the beliefs that have been running your thoughts, words and actions.

Begin with your first memory and check in on the highlights: the things that stand out for you. Remember that this is not meant to be your comprehensive memoir. You can write your memoir at another time!

Next Step

Now, review your beliefs that you wrote about and see how those beliefs impacted your story. For example: If you ever have self-sabotage then there was a fear of success underlying that sabotage. If you believe that Love hurts, how does that manifest in your daily life and relationships?

Do you have a photo of you when you were younger that you like? Get that picture so you can look at it during this next exercise. While looking at that younger version of yourself and standing in your integrity at this moment, what do you want to tell that younger self? Write a letter that is age- appropriate to your younger self, sharing your feelings, success, and reassuring that younger version that things worked out and you are doing great with even more amazing things in store for your future. Sometimes we all need some reassurance. Offer unconditional love and support to your younger self in the letter and be sure to sign the letter!

Dear _____,

_____

_____

_____

_____

_____

_____

_____

_____

_____

_____

_____

_____

_____

_____

I love you,

_____

Use your creative nature to draw

Draw a picture of your inner life with your non-dominant hand. What does your inner sanctuary or house look like? How does it feel? What colors are there? Now, I am aware that your non-dominant hand may not yield an art piece for a gallery and that is not the point. Using your non-dominant hand gives your inner self a voice, and your inner self has things to say. It is time you listen, and art is a great form of expression!

Words of Encouragement

Now, establish eye contact with yourself in a mirror or use your selfie mode on your phone. Look at your beautiful eyes, feel your presence with all the feelings and say, "This is for me because I deserve it." If you tear up, let them flow.

Now it is time to get into the process of this companion workbook and your soulful transformation:

<u>3</u>

THE PROCESS

Caring for Your Soul

In a world not built for neurodivergent souls, it is vitally important to be attentive to caring for your soul. This takes dedication and resolve often because we are easily distracted and may not realize how a lack of soulful self-care can cause life challenges. Our relationships suffer and our wellbeing suffers when we neglect ourselves. When the messages all around are ones of not being good enough or something being wrong, we must challenge those lies with the truth. The truth is you are perfect, whole, and complete, fully equipped to do the things that ought to be done by you. Our work is part of caring for our soul so we can flourish as intensely sensitive people in this often-insensitive world.

Create space that is protected and dedicated to your welfare and self-care. As you move through the book and the questions use some frames or affirmations to help your focus.

Here are some examples. You could create your own as well.

"I believe in me and my power to take care of my soul"

"My present moment is where my authentic personal power lies."

"I have the power to grow, change, and evolve"

"I love me. I am safe."

Add your own affirmations:

<hr>

<hr>

Compassion and Its Role in Your Care

I imagine you have lived your life being pushed and expected to go faster, be better, do more than others. You have been largely misunderstood or outright ignored. Maybe you have even been bullied because of your neurodivergence.

Compassion is the fuel for the care of your soul. Practically, compassion is about forgiving yourself for the grand adventure of being human with all the blunders, confusion, missed opportunities, and more. It means that you use compassion as the salve for the wounds and low gentle healing of old pains, so they no longer control your current life.

Just as you have compassion for a dear friend who is hurting, so too, you want to have compassion for you.

Gratitude's Role in Your Life

Gratitude has a vital role in the lives of people who wish to be happy and satisfied. There are three realms of gratitude.
- Gratitude for the things/experiences you desire
- Gratitude in the face of those things/experiences you do not desire
- Gratitude for gratitude's sake

A good practice is to say "Thank you" as you pass through all doorways. What you are doing is holding the mindset and consciousness of gratitude that then opens your heart and soul to be cared for in meaningful ways. You are saying "Thank you" without having to think of a thing or person, that thank you is one of soulful gratitude in general. It makes practice easy because you are not having to think of a thing or person.

How to Use This Companion Workbook

- Create a sensory-friendly space, soft lighting, stim toy, or something soothing to drink.
- Read a chapter from the book.
- Ponder the reflection questions and let your energy guide you. There is plenty of space for your expression and honoring your inner process.
- Write, draw, voice note, or collage whatever helps your thoughts take shape in this workbook or your journal.
- Reflect on the topics for each corresponding chapter in this book and document your answer in the most aligned way you feel in this moment.
- There are no deadlines or wrong answers. Follow your unique rhythm.
- This care for your soul is meant to nourish you and support you. Allow yourself to feel nurtured, supported, valuable, heard, and loved, because you are.

THE CHAPTERS 1-50

Read the chapter from the book *Care for the Neurodivergent Soul.* Ponder the reflection questions and now, write your thoughts about the questions in this workbook in the places that correspond to each chapter. Remember that this is a process, and you will notice yourself changing as you go. Be honest with yourself. Be gentle.

I see you, and I know the inner fears of peeking inside our carefully constructed personalities. This is why compassion and deep soulful care are required for your happiness, health, and success.

I am here to support you through this my writing, my *Someone Gets Me* podcast, and as a visionary mentor. I am walking along the path with you, and I believe that you are beautiful, lovable, and capable.

My Beginning

Take some time to write in this workbook where you are now as a way to honor and see your progress. Our memory changes over time so writing some of your thoughts about how you are feeling and engaging in the world will be helpful. You will find several places throughout this workbook to pause and reflect. It is in reflection that you are able to integrate new knowledge and awareness.

_____

_____

_____

_____

_____

_____

_____

_____

_____

_____

_____

_____

_____

_____

_____

_____

_____

_____

_____

PART 1

DIFFERENT BY DESIGN

CHAPTER 1

WHAT IS IMPORTANT TO NEURODIVERGENT PEOPLE

Your neurodivergent soul doesn't thrive on hustle, shame, or pressure. It thrives on resonance. What lights you up, an interest, novelty, passion, and challenge aren't luxuries. They are how your brain and spirit come alive. When you follow these core drivers, you don't just function, you flourish. This chapter is about naming, and what makes you feel fully alive and engaged.

I notice that my energy soars when I am immersed in…

....

....

....

....

....

....

....

....

....

....

....

....

....

....

One practical way I will protect these priorities in daily life is…

_____

_____

_____

_____

_____

_____

_____

_____

_____

_____

_____

_____

_____

Sometimes the best way to start is with someone present. Body doubling can ease initiation and soften overwhelm.

A task that feels easier when someone else is present is…

....

....

....

....

....

....

....

....

....

....

....

....

....

....

One safe person I could invite to co-work or body double with me is…

CHAPTER 2

WHAT IS NOT IMPORTANT TO NEURODIVERGENT PEOPLE

You are not lazy. You are not unmotivated. You are likely responding to environments that rely on fear, shame, or superficial rewards to drive behavior systems that often don't work for your neurodivergent brain. This chapter explores what doesn't move you and why rejecting misaligned motivators is essential for reclaiming your authentic momentum.

Rules, tasks, or expectations I'm ready to release because they drain me are...

....

....

....

....

....

....

....

....

....

....

....

....

When I give myself permission to ignore the unimportant, I feel…

_____

_____

_____

_____

_____

_____

_____

_____

_____

_____

_____

_____

_____

_____

You may find that your motivation flourishes through emotional connection rather than through feeling pressure. This is emotional anchoring, remembering why a task or goal matters to your soul.

Something I care deeply about that could reawaken my energy is…

_____

_____

_____

_____

_____

_____

_____

_____

_____

_____

_____

_____

One way I can reconnect emotionally to a current project is…

CHAPTER 3

THE CHALLENGES ARE VERY REAL

Living in a world not designed for your wiring means facing friction everywhere, from transitions and shutdowns to sensory overload and masking. Recognizing that the challenges are systemic, not personal, is a turning point. This chapter invites you to name your most pressing mismatches and begin rewriting the script with compassion.

The mismatch I struggle with most right now looks like…

....

....

....

....

....

....

....

....

....

....

....

....

....

....

....

....

....

A compassionate response I can offer myself in those moments is…

_____

_____

_____

_____

_____

_____

_____

_____

_____

_____

_____

_____

_____

_____

_____

_____

_____

_____

_____

_____

_____

_____

Shutdown isn't failure. It's your system saying, "I need refuge." A personalized recovery plan can help you return gently, without judgment.

My shutdown signs include…

....
....
....
....
....
....
....
....
....
....
....
....
....
....
....
....
....
....
....
....
....
....
....
....
....
....

What helps me recover gently is…

CHAPTER 4

HEALING ON MULTIPLE FRONTS

Recovery, Health Challenges, and Navigating Professional Help

Healing is not just about one area of your life; it's layered, interconnected. Neurodivergent healing must tend to body, mind, and soul, often in parallel. This chapter invites you to tune into what your system truly needs and assemble a support team that respects your unique rhythm.

My body is asking for support in the form of…

....

....

....

....

....

....

....

....

....

....

....

....

....

....

A professional or ally I feel drawn to invite onto my care team is...

Healing also includes co-regulation, being with people who help your nervous system feel safe. You don't have to do everything alone.

People or animals that help me feel safe are…

_____

_____

_____

_____

_____

_____

_____

_____

_____

_____

_____

_____

_____

_____

_____

_____

_____

_____

_____

_____

One way I can increase supportive contact this week is…

....

....

....

PART 2

THE GIFTED AND NEURODIVERGENT INTERSECTION

Journal Break

Take some time to write in this workbook where you are now as a way to honor and see your progress. Our memory changes over time so writing some of your thoughts about how you are feeling and engaging in the world will be helpful. You will find several places throughout this workbook to pause and reflect. It is in reflection that you are able to integrate new knowledge and awareness.

CHAPTER 5

THE POWERFUL AND FIERCE INTERSECTION

Giftedness and neurodivergence often show up hand in hand, intensities, sensitivities, fierce focus, and emotional depth. This intersection is a source of creative fire, insight, and intuition. It is not a flaw as we sometimes believe. It is time to change our own perceptions of our own uniqueness.

The superpower that emerges from my unique wiring is…

_____

_____

_____

_____

_____

_____

Today I will celebrate that power by…

_____

_____

_____

_____

_____

Gifted neurodivergence often means a mind that never stops and a heart that feels everything. Creativity is one way to honor and channel that depth.

When I create freely, I feel…

_____

_____

_____

_____

_____

_____

One playful or expressive act I want to explore this month is…

_____

_____

_____

_____

_____

_____

_____

_____

_____

_____

_____

_____

CHAPTER 6

A SOUL IN NEED OF CARE

Even the most visionary soul gets tired. Craving solitude, silence, or softness means your nervous system is asking for care. When you are feeling weary or worn down, it doesn't mean you're failing; it does mean that it is time for some care.

Signals that my soul is craving gentler care include…

....

....

....

....

....

....

....

The most nourishing practice I can offer myself this week is…

....

....

....

....

....

....

....

....

....

CHAPTER 7

DEFINING "CARE" BEYOND PRODUCTIVITY

Care is something you need and deserve, not something you earn. When you are uniquely wired for depth, stillness can feel radical. In this chapter, you'll redefine care in your own terms, not tied to how much you accomplish or how hard you work.

Care that feels good to me, even if it looks unproductive is…

....

....

....

....

....

....

One belief about worth and productivity I'm ready to retire is…

....

....

....

....

....

....

CHAPTER 8

HOW TO CHASE BIG DREAMS WITHOUT MELTING DOWN

Dreaming big doesn't have to mean burning out. The goal is to pursue what excites you without losing access to your regulation, rest, and joy. Let your goals stretch you without severing your self-connection.

My big, sparkly dream is…

....
....
....
....
....
....

I will safeguard my nervous system on the journey by…

....
....
....
....
....

CHAPTER 9

THE RHYTHM OF YOUR ENERGY IS UNIQUELY YOU

Your personal daily, weekly, monthly and annual rhythms are unique to you and often follow the seasons. You weren't meant to move at society's pace. Your rhythms may come in bursts, dips, or cycles. Recognizing and honoring this flow is an act of self-respect and nervous system safety.

My natural peak-focus times of day feel like…

....
....
....
....
....
....

I can honor those rhythms tomorrow by…

....
....
....
....
....

The season(s) I feel most alive in is…

_____

_____

_____

_____

_____

_____

_____

_____

_____

_____

_____

_____

_____

_____

_____

_____

_____

_____

_____

_____

_____

_____

_____

_____

_____

CHAPTER 10

THE SACRED POWER OF SAYING NO

"No" is a complete sentence. Saying "no" is not rejection, rather it is a healthy boundary. Learning to say no helps you build a life that aligns with your energy, values, and capacity. It's an anchor, not a shutdown.

A recent "yes" that should have been a "no" was…

....

....

....

....

....

....

....

Next time, I will protect my energy by…

....

....

....

....

....

....

....

CHAPTER 11

THE ART OF SUSTAINABLE CONTRIBUTION

Sustainable contribution means offering your gifts in a way that honors your capacity, not drains it. You don't need to burn out to make an impact. Contribution can be small, sacred, and still powerful.

Causes or communities that light me up are…

_____

_____

_____

_____

_____

_____

A bite-sized, sustainable way I can contribute is…

_____

_____

_____

_____

_____

_____

_____

_____

CHAPTER 12

THE NECESSITY OF JOY AND PLAY

Joy and play are nervous system nutrients. They are not distractions. Making space for many kinds of play is how you recover your creativity, connection, and resilience.

When I allow myself to play, I notice…

_____

_____

_____

_____

_____

_____

A playful activity I will schedule this week is…

_____

_____

_____

_____

_____

_____

CHAPTER 13

THE QUIET POWER OF SOLITUDE

Solitude is a form of restoration. For many neurodivergent folks, intentional time alone is where your healing, clarity, and brilliance emerge through the chaos and distractions of everyday life. Quiet solitude is a protected and dedicated time apart which is quite different than being lonely.

Solitude restores me by…

....
....
....
....
....
....

I will create a pocket of protected time of intentional solitude by…

....
....
....
....
....

PART 3

UNDERSTANDING THE NEURODIVERGENT SOUL

Journal Break

Take some time to write in this workbook where you are now as a way to honor and see your progress. Our memory changes over time so writing some of your thoughts about how you are feeling and engaging in the world will be helpful. You will find several places throughout this workbook to pause and reflect. It is in reflection that you are able to integrate new knowledge and awareness.

_____

_____

_____

_____

_____

_____

_____

_____

_____

_____

_____

_____

_____

_____

_____

_____

_____

_____

_____

_____

_____

_____

CHAPTER 14

INTRICATE MINDS: GIFTEDNESS, ADHD & AUTISM

Your mind is layered and multidimensional. Giftedness, ADHD, and autism often overlap, creating complexity that demands compassion. When you get caught up in the comparison conversation, you will often find yourself comparing aspects that do not correlate, so comparison can be limiting and even dangerous at times.

The overlap I see in my own mind between creativity and neurodivergence is…

....

....

....

....

....

I will honor that intricacy through…

....

....

....

....

CHAPTER 15

LIVING IN A WORLD NOT BUILT FOR YOU

You are not too much. The world is too narrow. This chapter is about naming the spaces that don't work and empowering yourself to navigate, reshape, or exit them.

A setting that drains me because it isn't designed for my needs is…

....

....

....

....

....

....

....

A modification or advocacy step I can try is…

....

....

....

....

....

....

....

CHAPTER 16

SENSORY SENSITIVITY AND THE SOUL

Sensory processing is more than a physical experience; it is spiritual and energetic. Your sensory profile holds clues to what brings comfort, overwhelm, and peace to your Soul.

My most tender sensory channel is…

....

....

....

....

....

....

A soothing tool, texture, or sound that comforts me is…

....

....

....

....

....

....

....

....

CHAPTER 17

EMOTIONAL DEPTH, EMPATHY & OVERWHELM

You feel deeply and that is a gift. Healthy and meaningful boundaries and rituals honor your empathy and emotional depth. Overwhelm can leave you depleted. This chapter is about loving yourself and life itself without leaking.

When my empathy feels overwhelming, my body tells me by…

....

....

....

....

....

A boundary or ritual that helps me stay centered is…

....

....

....

....

....

....

CHAPTER 18

THE MYTH OF BROKENNESS: UNLEARNING INTERNALIZED ABLEISM

You are not broken. You are brilliant and different by design. Let's release the labels and stories that suggest otherwise.

One "too much" label I'm ready to release is…

....

....

....

....

....

....

I will affirm my wholeness today by…

....

....

....

....

PART 4

RESTORING YOUR INNER WORLD

Journal Break

Take some time to write in this workbook where you are now as a way to honor and see your progress. Our memory changes over time, so writing some of your thoughts about how you are feeling and engaging in the world will be helpful. You will find several places throughout this workbook to pause and reflect. It is in reflection that you are able to integrate new knowledge and awareness.

_____

_____

_____

_____

_____

_____

_____

_____

_____

_____

_____

_____

_____

_____

_____

_____

_____

_____

_____

_____

CHAPTER 19

RECLAIMING THE SELF AFTER TRAUMA

Trauma can fracture your identity. Recovery is the act of remembering who you were before the world told you to shrink. Recovery means to "feel better." Part of feeling better is reclaiming those parts of us that we left behind during traumatic and chaotic times.

A way I can create personal safety is…

_____

_____

_____

_____

_____

A fragment of myself I'm welcoming back is…

_____

_____

_____

_____

_____

The safest place for that part to land is…

....

....

....

....

....

....

....

CHAPTER 20

EMBRACING REST AS RADICAL CARE

Rest is your right. Some people think that rest is some sort of reward for doing lots of work, but this is a limited viewpoint. Practicing deep rest is an act of resistance to the status quo and reverence for you and your essence.

Rest feels radical to me because…

....
....
....
....
....
....
....

I will gift myself one unapologetic rest moment by…

....
....
....
....
....
....
....

CHAPTER 21

REPAIRING YOUR INNER DIALOGUE

The way you speak to yourself becomes the soil of your healing. This chapter supports you in replacing harshness with self-compassion.

Find a quiet corner, light a candle, and speak aloud your new truth.

A harsh phrase I often tell myself is...

....

....

....

....

....

....

....

I will rewrite it into a kinder truth ...

....

....

....

....

....

....

....

CHAPTER 22

SENSORY SANCTUARIES: CREATING SPACES THAT SOOTHE

Your environment can either agitate or regulate your nervous system. This chapter invites you to build your own sensory sanctuary.

Play ambient music or bring a soft object to your journaling space.

A corner of my home I could transform into a sensory haven is…

....

....

....

....

....

....

Items that would make it cozier include…

....

....

....

....

CHAPTER 23

THE ART OF SLOWING DOWN

Slowing down is how you listen to your soul. It might feel unfamiliar at first, but it's where your truth lives.

Turn off notifications and let this journaling be tech-free if possible.

Slowing down scares me when…

....

....

....

....

....

....

Today I will practice slow living by…

....

....

....

....

....

....

CHAPTER 24

RITUALS FOR REGULATION

Rituals are anchors in chaos. They don't need to be perfect or fancy, just consistent and meaningful.

Wrap yourself in a blanket or use rhythmic breathing before you begin.

My go-to quick regulation ritual is…

_____

_____

_____

_____

_____

_____

_____

I'd like to experiment with adding…

_____

_____

_____

_____

_____

_____

_____

CHAPTER 25

CREATIVITY AS SELF-SOOTHING

Creativity is not just for artists. It's a way of processing, soothing, and celebrating your aliveness.

Keep art supplies, soft pens, or color markers nearby to doodle as you reflect.

When I create, I notice my nervous system feels…

....

....

....

....

....

....

A tiny, low-pressure creative act I can try this week is…

....

....

....

....

....

....

CHAPTER 26

WHAT RESISTANCE SAYS ABOUT YOUR NEEDS

Resistance isn't laziness, it's wisdom. It often points to unmet needs or inner conflict. Listen before you push.

Give yourself permission to pause. Journal after a short walk or deep breath.

Lately, resistance shows up as…

....
....
....
....
....
....

If I listen closely, it's asking me to…

....
....
....
....
....
....

CHAPTER 27

BUILDING A SAFE INNER SANCTUARY

Your inner sanctuary is where your truth is always welcome. This chapter supports building that space inside you.

Close your eyes and imagine a safe place before you write. Let your body relax.

A visualization that instantly grounds me is…

....

....

....

....

....

....

I will return to this sanctuary when…

....

....

....

....

....

....

PART 5

PURPOSE WITHOUT BURNOUT

Journal Break

Take some time to write in this workbook where you are now as a way to honor and see your progress. Our memory changes over time so writing some of your thoughts about how you are feeling and engaging in the world will be helpful. You will find several places throughout this workbook to pause and reflect. It is in reflection that you are able to integrate new knowledge and awareness.

CHAPTER 28

THE PRESSURE TO BE EXTRAORDINARY

You don't have to be exceptional to be worthy. Let go of the grind and choose meaning over performance.

Soften your posture. Stretch, then reflect with your hand on your heart.

The narrative that I must always excel sounds like…

....
....
....
....
....
....

I choose to redefine "extraordinary" as…

....
....
....
....
....

CHAPTER 29

RETHINKING PRODUCTIVITY AND WORTH

You are not a machine. Productivity doesn't define your worth. This chapter invites you to decouple the two.

Place a soothing object nearby, a plant, stone, or soft fabric to anchor yourself.

My worth is inherently mine because…

....
....
....
....
....

A productivity rule that I am ready to re-write is…

....
....
....
....
....

CHAPTER 30

NAVIGATING SPECIAL INTERESTS AND HYPERFOCUS

Your special interests are sacred. Hyperfocus can be both a gift and a challenge. You will want to learn how to honor it without losing balance.

Keep a timer nearby or take breaks as you reflect on what pulls your focus with joy.

A special interest that feels like pure joy is…

....

....

....

....

....

I will honor its pull while safeguarding balance by…

....

....

....

....

....

CHAPTER 31

HOW TO CHASE BIG DREAMS WITHOUT MELTING DOWN

Return to your dreams often, but gently. Build safeguards that let you expand without collapsing.

Create a '"ream ritual." Light a candle, sip tea, journal about your next small step.

One boundary that will keep my big dream sustainable is…

....

....

....

....

....

....

The smallest next step I can joyfully take is…

....

....

....

....

....

....

CHAPTER 32

SUCCESS DYSPHORIA: WHEN ACHIEVEMENT FEELS EMPTY

Sometimes success doesn't feel like you thought it would. That doesn't mean you failed. It means your heart is asking for something deeper.

Breathe into your belly. Ask yourself gently: what was I truly hoping success would give me?

An achievement that left me unexpectedly hollow was…

....
....
....
....
....

What my heart was truly craving then was…

....
....
....
....
....

CHAPTER 33

SUSTAINABLE PURPOSE: YOUR RIGHT TO A GENTLE LIFE

Your life's work can be fierce and gentle at once. You don't have to sacrifice peace to live with purpose.

Wrap yourself in something soft or write in a quiet, sunlit space if you can.

A gentle, purpose-filled life looks like…

....

....

....

....

....

One gentle practice I will weave into tomorrow is…

....

....

....

....

....

....

PART 6

SOUL CARE AS A LIFELONG PRACTICE

Journal Break

Take some time to write in this workbook where you are now as a way to honor and see your progress. Our memory changes over time so writing some of your thoughts about how you are feeling and engaging in the world will be helpful. You will find several places throughout this workbook to pause and reflect. It is in reflection that you are able to integrate new knowledge and awareness.

....

....

....

....

....

....

....

....

....

....

....

....

....

....

....

....

....

....

CHAPTER 34

CYCLES OF ENERGY AND SHUTDOWN

Your energy is not linear. It cycles. Shutdowns are not weaknesses, they are signals. This chapter invites awareness and grace.

Reflect after rest. Use low lighting or calming scents to stay grounded while writing.

A recent shutdown moment taught me that…

_____

_____

_____

_____

_____

_____

In my next low-energy phase, I will…

_____

_____

_____

_____

_____

CHAPTER 35

SOUL ANCHORS - PRACTICES THAT REGULATE & RENEW

Soul anchors are practices that bring you back into balance. They regulate and restore you when the world feels overwhelming.

List your favorite anchors while listening to soft instrumental music or in a cozy sensory space.

My most reliable soul anchor is…

....
....
....
....
....

I will refresh this anchor by…

....
....
....
....
....

CHAPTER 36

REDEFINING RESILIENCE - HEALING ON YOUR OWN TERMS

Resilience is not about enduring harm. It's about reshaping your life so that you heal gently, in your way.

Take grounding breaths before journaling to embody resilience as soft strength.

Resilience, for me, now means…

....

....

....

....

....

I honor my personalized resilience by…

....

....

....

....

....

CHAPTER 37

SPIRITUALITY BEYOND DOGMA

Your spirit deserves freedom beyond rigid rules. This chapter invites you to discover what feels deeply authentic.

Hold an object of meaning (stone, candle, fabric) while writing.

A spiritual practice that feels authentically mine is...

....
....
....
....
....
....

I will nurture it this week by...

....
....
....
....
....
....
....

CHAPTER 38

REBUILDING TRUST WITH YOUR NERVOUS SYSTEM

Your nervous system needs to know you'll listen. Trust builds through small moments of care and response.

Breathe deeply and place your hand on your heart before writing.

My body says "trust me" when…

....

....

....

....

....

....

I will demonstrate trust by…

....

....

....

....

....

....

CHAPTER 39

DESIGNING A LIFE THAT HONORS YOUR ENERGY

Instead of forcing yourself into others' timelines, design life around your energy patterns.

Write while noticing how your energy feels right now.

One daily chore I can tailor to my energy pattern is…

....
....
....
....
....
....

A supportive tool or technology that can help is…

....
....
....
....
....

CHAPTER 40

CHOOSING A LIFE YOU DON'T HAVE TO RECOVER FROM

A life of constant recovery is unsustainable. This chapter supports creating a life where daily living feels nourishing.

Wrap up in a blanket or soft fabric to symbolize gentleness.

A recurring obligation I'm ready to release or redesign is…

....
....
....
....
....
....

The freedom I imagine on the other side feels like…

....
....
....
....
....
....

CHAPTER 41

THE SACRED ACT OF UNMASKING

Unmasking is sacred, it allows your true self to emerge in safety and love.

Visualize a trusted space where you are fully yourself before journaling.

A small way I can unmask safely today is…

....
....
....
....
....
....
....

A trusted person or place where I feel free to be unmasked is…

....
....
....
....
....
....

CHAPTER 42

WRITING YOUR OWN DEFINITION OF SUCCESS

Redefining success on your terms ensures your life aligns with your soul, not external pressure.

Play a song that makes you feel powerful as you write.

Success, in my language, looks and feels like…

....

....

....

....

....

....

I will measure it through…

....

....

....

....

....

....

CHAPTER 43

THE PRACTICE OF SELF-COMPASSION

Self-compassion transforms your inner dialogue. It's not indulgence, it is essential care.

Journal with a soothing presence nearby like a candle or gentle soundscape.

The tone of voice my inner critic uses is…

....
....
....
....
....
....
....

Today, I respond with compassionate words such as…

....
....
....
....
....
....

CHAPTER 44

BELONGING TO YOURSELF

Belonging begins with yourself. No external approval can replace it.

Reflect outdoors or in solitude to anchor your sense of self-belonging.

I feel most like I belong to myself when…

....
....
....
....
....
....

A boundary that safeguards that belonging is…

....
....
....
....
....
....
....

CHAPTER 45

YOU ARE DOING THE WORK - RECEIVE THE LIFE YOU IMAGINE

You have tended to your healing. Now allow yourself to receive the fruits of your effort, joy, rest, and fulfillment.

Breathe gratitude into your body before writing.

Evidence that my inner work is already blooming is…

....

....

....

....

....

....

I will allow myself to receive by…

....

....

....

....

....

PART 7

NAVIGATING RELATIONSHIPS

Journal Break

Take some time to write in this workbook where you are now as a way to honor and see your progress. Our memory changes over time so writing some of your thoughts about how you are feeling and engaging in the world will be helpful. You will find several places throughout this workbook to pause and reflect. It is in reflection that you are able to integrate new knowledge and awareness.

CHAPTER 46

LONELINESS AND THE SEARCH FOR KINDRED SPIRITS

Loneliness is real, but so is connection. Seek the kindred spirits who resonate with your essence.

Visualize the qualities of a kindred spirit while journaling.

Qualities I long for in kindred spirits include…

....

....

....

....

....

....

I will take one brave step toward connection by…

....

....

....

....

....

CHAPTER 47

BOUNDARIES FOR THE HYPER-EMPATHIC SOUL

Deep empathy requires boundaries to protect your own emotional landscape.

Imagine a gentle shield of light around you while you reflect.

A recent moment I absorbed someone else's feelings was…

....
....
....
....
....
....

The boundary that would protect my energy next time is…

....
....
....
....
....
....

CHAPTER 48

FINDING YOUR NEURODIVERGENT COMMUNITY

Community heals isolation. Find places where your neurodivergence is celebrated.

Hold an item that represents community or belonging.

Spaces where my neurodivergence feels celebrated include…

_____

_____

_____

_____

_____

_____

I will explore a new community option by…

_____

_____

_____

_____

_____

CHAPTER 49

LOVE IN TRANSLATION - INTIMACY WITH A DIFFERENT OPERATING SYSTEM

Intimacy across neurotypes requires compassion and translation. It's a bridge-building act.

Reflect on how you give and receive love, while holding a comforting object.

A communication bridge that helps my relationships is…

....
....
....
....
....

I will lovingly explain my needs by saying…

....
....
....
....
....

CHAPTER 50

SAFETY IN NEURODIVERGENT RELATIONSHIPS

Safety is essential for love and friendship. This chapter affirms the importance of co-creating emotional security.

Picture a safe relational space as you journal.

I feel emotionally safe when my partner/friend…

....
....
....
....
....
....
....

I will contribute to mutual safety by…

....
....
....
....
....

Closing Reflection: You Are Not Alone

Take some time to write in this workbook where you are now as a way to honor and see your progress. Our memory changes over time so writing some of your thoughts about how you are feeling and engaging in the world will be helpful. You will find several places throughout this workbook to pause and reflect. It is in reflection that you are able to integrate new knowledge and awareness.

Letter to Your Future Self

Take a moment and sit comfortably and close your eyes. Breathe deeply and feel yourself become aligned within. Imagine the best version of yourself about a year or two from this moment. What is happening in your life? What are you engaged with day to day? What excites you? What challenges or hurdles have you overcome? Take some time to nurture your innermost self.

Let this final page be a letter to your future self. Offer your wisdom, care, and hope.

I, _____, hereby pledge to move through life with passion, and I envision and create my life with an open heart and an open mind. I am committed to my process and carrying forward my insights that I have gathered along my journey.

I want you to remember …

_____

_____

_____

_____

_____

_____

_____

_____

_____

_____

_____

I commit to protecting and celebrating my neurodivergent soul by…

....

....

....

....

....

....

....

....

....

....

....

As I continue self-reflection, I am intentional in my ongoing commitment to caring deeply for my neurodivergent soul.

_____
Signature

_____
Date

Epilogue

You've shown up. You've reflected. You have told yourself the truth.

This matters.

Every word you have written, every page you have sat with, and every time you chose presence over perfection, you built something. You are not starting from scratch. You're starting from strength, experience and wisdom.

Your soul care is working. Your rhythm is valid. Your energy is precious.

This workbook has been your companion, and the real transformation is happening in you. It is in the way you are choosing rest, connection, honesty, boundaries, creativity, joy, and your own timing. That is the work. That is your win.

You already carry the wisdom you have been seeking. You already are the person you have been trying to become.

Your journey continues with new awareness, deeper compassion, and greater trust in yourself. There is no finish line to cross, simply layer after layer of becoming more fully you. You are already enough.

Keep honoring your design. Keep choosing what nourishes you. Keep living from the truth of your neurodivergent brilliance.

You are ready. You are radiant. You are a force. I am so proud of the way you are showing up for your one extraordinary life.

With deep love and fierce belief in you,

Dianne

About the Author

Dianne A. Allen, MA is a visionary mentor, intuitive guide, and ambassador for gifted and neurodivergent adults, families, and teams. With decades of experience as a counselor, speaker, and author, Dianne blends emotional wisdom with grounded expertise to help others reconnect with their innate brilliance. As the founder of *Someone Gets Me* and *Visions Applied*, she empowers sensitive, creative, and high-achieving individuals to embrace their full selves and thrive in a world that often misunderstands them.

Known for her compassionate clarity and soulful insight, Dianne's work bridges the seen and unseen, the scientific and the spiritual. Her writing, speaking, and mentoring illuminate a path of deep self-trust, restoration, and lasting transformation. Through *Care for the Neurodivergent Soul Companion Workbook*, she offers both a sanctuary and a guidebook for those longing to feel seen, heard, and fully alive.

Connect with Dianne:
www.MsDianneAllen.com
www.VisionsApplied.com
www.retreatwithdianne.com

Previous Books include:
How to Quit Anything in 5 Simple Steps
The Loneliness Cure
Daily Meditations for Visionary Leaders
Hope Realized
Where Do You Fit In?
Someone Gets Me
Care for The Neurodivergent Soul

Protected and Dedicated Journaling Environment

Investing in creating a dedicated safe space for your journaling is a vital part of your self-care. Here are some suggestions and things to ponder when creating your sacred journaling environment.

Inner Environment

Hydration – Being well hydrated is important. Clearing out the old and birthing and tending to the new requires energy. Water is needed more than ever when you are making life changes.

Nutrition – Eat healthy foods and take the time to chew your food. Eating on the run or not eating works against your success.

Mindset – Cultivate a mindset that empowers you and your dedication to nurturing your soul. Use affirmations or frames to act as powerful reminders.

Belief Systems – 75% of your belief systems are instilled before the age of 2. Many are non-verbal and only become apparent as adults when we run into them. As you grow and transform, you will be afforded the opportunity to identify, reflect upon and choose how to respond to your beliefs. Keep it, lose it or change it. The choice is always yours.

Outer Environment

Temperature- Being too hot or too cold can create challenges for you. Be sure to create a temperature in your space that is welcoming and soothing for you.

Ambiance – You may desire total quiet or white noise or background sounds like tv, or music. This may change based on what you are journaling as well as your feelings at the time. Be gentle with yourself and honor your needs and desires.

Lighting – Use lighting that is conducive to your mood and style. When your intense sensitivities are triggered, journaling can be harder, and you may not even want to get started. Make your space comfortable.

Comfort – Comfortable clothing, comfortable furniture, and comfortable sitting positions are important. You may enjoy a weighted blanket. What feels comfortable may change over time with the seasons or your personal changes. Allow flexibility and honor yourself as you change.

Writing Instrument – Your writing instrument is crucial. Handwriting is much healthier for your brain than typing so I suggest a great pen or pencil that feels nice. The kind of utensil, its weight and feel are very important. I bet you have a special pen or pencil that works best for you. If you do not, take a trip to an office supply store and try out different instruments and choose one that feels divine!

Journal – What you are writing in is also important. The thickness, color, and texture of the paper in addition to how the journal is bound all makes a difference.

Scents – Do you enjoy certain scents or aromatherapy? Your olfactory sense is very sensitive and can assist in your journaling by offering comfort, safety, inspiration, motivation and more.

A Resource Guide for the Neurodivergent Soul

This collection of resources is designed to support your ongoing journey. Whether you are seeking deeper knowledge, meaningful community, or compassionate tools for daily life, these offerings provide pathways to continued care, clarity, and connection. These resources are not prescriptive checklists, they are invitations. Take what resonates. Leave what doesn't. Add your own discoveries. Most of all, let your inner wisdom guide you as you continue honoring your path.

Books by Dianne A. Allen

These works form the heart of the message carried throughout *Care for the Neurodivergent Soul*. They are written for the gifted, the intense, the sensitive, and the seekers who long to be seen and understood.

- *Care for the Neurodivergent Soul*
- *Someone Gets Me.* A compassionate guide for gifted, ADHD, and autistic adults navigating a world not designed for them. This book offers validation, soulful insight, and practical tools for healing and thriving.
- *Where Do You Fit In?* Written especially for those who feel "different on purpose," this book provides clarity and direction for gifted souls seeking connection without compromising who they are.
- *Hope Realized.* A collection of daily reflections with journaling prompts for those who are healing their heart, soul, and inner knowing.
- *Meditations for Visionary Leaders.* A collection of daily reflections for those who lead from the heart, soul, and inner knowing.
- *The Loneliness Cure: A Guide to Contentment.* Explores the hidden struggles of intelligent, sensitive, and gifted adults who

often feel out of place despite their external success. Offers practical guidance and hopeful reflection on cultivating true belonging.

- *How to Quit Anything in 5 Simple Steps*. Seeks to explore ways to become free of addictive patterns using a multifaceted model for regaining life balance and freedom.

Further Reading for the Neurodivergent Soul

- *The Divergent Mind*, by Jenara Nerenberg. A groundbreaking book on neurodivergent women and nonbinary individuals and their experience of sensitivity, creativity, and intuition.
- *Neurotribes*, by Steve Silberman. An expansive history of autism and the evolution of neurodiversity. Offers cultural context and advocacy insights.
- *Drama of the Gifted Child*, by Alice Miller. A classic on the emotional challenges of gifted children and the importance of reclaiming the authentic self.
- *Quiet: The Power of Introverts in a World That Can't Stop Talking*, by Susan Cain. A powerful resource for sensitive and introspective souls navigating a noisy world.
- *Uniquely Human*, by Barry M. Prizant, PhD. Shifts the lens on autism from pathology to humanity, offering compassionate understanding.
- *Neurodiversity Playbook: How Neurodivergent People Can Crack the Code of Living in a Neurotypical World*, by Matthew Zakreski, PsyD. This book represents a summation of a decade's worth of therapy, research, workshops, and presentations around the unique aspects of social-emotional development in the neurodivergent community.
- *Gifted and Distractible: Understanding, Supporting, and Advocating for Your Twice Exceptional Child*, by Julie F. Skolnick. A practical, research-based guide that demystifies giftedness and learning differences to help "twice exceptional" children thrive.

Podcasts

- *Someone Gets Me*, with Dianne A. Allen. A podcast for gifted, sensitive, and neurodivergent individuals exploring authenticity, intuition, creativity, and leadership. Features interviews, reflections, and practical tools for soulful living. Listen on Apple Podcasts or Spotify
- *The Neurodiversity Podcast* (formerly *The Mind Matters Podcast*). Hosted by Emily Kircher-Morris, LPC, this show offers expert conversations on twice-exceptionality, giftedness, ADHD, autism, and education.
- *Uniquely Human: The Podcast.* Hosted by Dr. Barry Prizant and Dave Finch, this podcast explores autism and neurodiversity with warmth, insight, and humor.
- *The Divergent Mind Podcast.* Conversations about living and thriving as a neurodivergent adult, with emphasis on self-discovery, boundaries, and identity.
- *Embracing Intensity.* A blog and podcast for gifted, creative, and intense adults who are often misunderstood. Includes community events and self-discovery workbooks. **https://www.embracingintensity.com**
- *Nerding out on Neurodiversity.* A podcast hosted by Dr. Matt Zakreski, PsyD. You will be inspired and feel seen. **https://open.spotify.com/show/2XX6vKYjx2Ih4fAaTdU3Bd**

Websites and Online Communities

- Visions Applied. Home of Dianne A. Allen's mentoring, books, and programs. Offers one-on-one guidance, soulful resources, and community for gifted and neurodivergent adults. www.visionsapplied.com
- Ms Dianne Allen. Offers several unique programs and custom offerings from Dianne. Offering intuitive mentoring, consulting, guidance, and support for gifted and neurodivergent

individuals within the corporate, entrepreneur space, or families. www.msdianneallen.com
- Dr. Matt Zakreski. A seasoned clinical psychologist and speaker, Dr. Matt Zakreski is known for transforming the lives of audiences. His talks are attended by people of all ages and backgrounds and have inspired leaders from a variety of industries. Dr. Zakreski combines a strategic approach with an outside-the-box perspective to help you breakthrough challenges and reach your goals. www.drmattzakreski.com
- With Understanding Comes Calm. Offers resources and community for parents and adults navigating giftedness, twice-exceptionality, and mental health. www.withunderstandingcomescalm.com
- The Neurodivergent Woman. Empowering and educational resource for late-diagnosed neurodivergent women. Also has a podcast of the same name. https://theneurodivergentwoman.com
- Gifted and Distractible (With Bright & Quirky). Offers resources and community for parents and adults navigating giftedness, twice-exceptionality, and mental health. www.brightandquirky.com
- SENG (Supporting Emotional Needs of the Gifted). A leading organization focused on the social and emotional needs of gifted individuals. Offers parent groups, adult resources, and events. **www.sengifted.org**
- ADDA (Attention Deficit Disorder Association). Offers resources for adults with ADHD, including webinars, virtual support groups, and advocacy tools. **www.add.org**
- AuDHD.org. A hub for those who identify as both autistic and ADHD, providing affirming resources, blog posts, and lived experience narratives. **www.audhd.org**
- Focusmate.com. A virtual body doubling and co-working platform that gives you someone to work alongside when you need someone to connect with.

Tools & Sensory-Friendly Resources

- **Loop Earplugs**. Designed for sound sensitivity; these stylish and effective earplugs help regulate overwhelming environments. **www.loopearplugs.com**
- **Time Timer®**. A visual timer that helps with executive functioning, time-blindness, and transitions, particularly useful for ADHD individuals. **www.timetimer.com**
- **Insight Timer (App)**. A free meditation and mindfulness app with guided practices, music, and tools for sleep and nervous system regulation. **www.insighttimer.com**
- **EmWave by HeartMath**. A biofeedback tool that supports emotional regulation and coherence by tracking heart rhythms. **www.heartmath.com**

Reflection and Integration Tools (Printable or Editable)

These tools are available through *Care for the Neurodivergent Soul* or via the Visions Applied resource hub:

- **Energy Map Worksheet**. A one-page guide to help track and honor your energy rhythm throughout the day or week.
- **Daily Rhythm Template**. Designed with neurodivergent needs in mind, this tool helps you build a sustainable, sensory-aware daily flow.
- **Coming Home to Your Inner Compass**. A short, guided practice for reconnecting with your intuitive self and calming the nervous system.
- **Reflection Journal Prompts**. Printable prompts for deeper self-exploration, aligned with themes throughout the book.

You are not alone in this transformation. Others have walked and are walking their own neurodivergent soul path. Together, we remember how to live fully, love freely, and lead from the truth of who we are.

Personal Journal

www.ingramcontent.com/pod-product-compliance
Lightning Source LLC
Chambersburg PA
CBHW071512120626
46550CB00006B/2202